Bad Guys and Gals
of the WILD WEST

Dona Herweck Rice

Consultants

Timothy Rasinski, Ph.D.
Kent State University

Lori Oczkus
Literacy Consultant

Marcus McArthur, Ph.D
Department of History,
Saint Louis University

Based on writing from
TIME For Kids. TIME For Kids and the *TIME For Kids* logo are registered trademarks of TIME Inc. Used under license.

Publishing Credits

Dona Herweck Rice, *Editor-in-Chief*
Lee Aucoin, *Creative Director*
Jamey Acosta, *Senior Editor*
Robin Erckson, *Designer*
Stephanie Reid, *Photo Editor*
Rachelle Cracchiolo, *M.S.Ed., Publisher*

Image Credits: cover The Granger Collection; pp.16, 19 (bottom), 22, 23, 25 (top), 37 (top), Everett Collage Fotostock; pp.46 Walter Bibikow/age Fotostock; pp.24, 25 (left), 28, 30, 36, 37 (bottom), 44, 47, 53 The Bridgeman Art Library; pp.18, 19 (top), 29, 42 Corbis; pp.9 (top center) 25 (right), 31, 39 Getty Images; p.32 Kathy Walsh/Flickr; p.57 Meade County Historical Society; pp.1, 20, 21, 26, 49 The Granger Collection; pp.7 (top), 9 (top left to right bottom); 17 (bottom), 27, 34, 40, 43, 45, 52, 56 The Library of Congress; pp.9–12, 14–15, 54–55 (illustrations) Timothy J. Bradley; All other images from Shutterstock.

Teacher Created Materials

5301 Oceanus Drive
Huntington Beach, CA 92649-1030
http://www.tcmpub.com

ISBN 978-1-4333-4903-4
© 2013 Teacher Created Materials, Inc.

Table of Contents

Bad?

In the movie *Who Framed Roger Rabbit?*, the cartoon character Jessica Rabbit famously says, "I'm not bad. I'm just drawn that way." She means that appearances can be **deceiving**. The detective in the movie misjudges Jessica, and the "bad guy" nearly gets away. Jessica isn't bad at all.

The way a person looks may make you think he or she is up to no good. But is it fair to judge? Should you trust your **instincts** just to be safe? And who gets to decide what's bad—or good—anyway?

It's also true that someone can look perfectly nice and be a terribly bad guy—or gal.

◆ What was life like in the Wild West?
◆ Why were there so many bad guys and gals in the Wild West?
◆ Who were some of the most **notorious** figures from this time?

The Long Arm of the Law

If a person breaks the law, does that make him or her bad? What if the law is one of the following "strange but true" laws? These laws are so old and unusual that very few people even know about them!

• In one California town, it is against the law to wear cowboy boots unless you own at least two cows.

• In a community in Kentucky, a married woman needs her husband's approval to buy a hat.

• In a North Carolina town, it is against the law for dogs and cats to fight.

• In one Maine community, a person cannot walk down the street while playing the violin.

5

Life in the Wild West

Turn on the TV today and you can probably find an old movie set in the Wild West, with sheriffs and gunslingers, cowboys and cattle **barons**, **pioneers** and American Indians, horses and cattle. Often there are gun battles, and people seem to be in danger daily.

Well, the truth is, that's only a part of what life was really like in the Wild West. Because there were few people spread out across wide areas, and there was very little **established** law, people could easily be in danger. But most days in the Wild West were the same as the others, filled with work, dirt, and more than a little boredom.

Still, just as in the movies, there were some colorful characters in the Wild West, and they weren't always on the right side of The Law. These are the "bad guys and gals" of the Wild West.

Horses were the fastest way to travel in the Wild West.

Wild West

The Wild West refers to life and times in the United States **frontier**, west of the Mississippi River, before a system of law was fully in place. The Wild West loosely covers the time from the early to late 1800s, although most people think of it as the period between the 1840s and 1900.

Life as a cowboy was hard and dangerous. Being dragged by a horse was the most common cause of death.

SHERIFF'S OFFICE

Sometimes, life in the Wild West really was wild. People had to defend themselves and couldn't count on The Law to do it for them.

BAD-TO-WORSE TIME LINE

The West was filled with kind people. But it's often the most notorious people we remember best.

Although "the Wild West" is a common phrase, most of these outlaws were born in the east and moved west.

Belle Starr
1848–1889

Jesse James
1847–1882

Doc Holliday
1851–1887

Gold Rush

When gold was discovered at Sutter's Mill in California in 1848, word spread quickly. People everywhere decided to take a chance and mine for gold. Many people braved the journey west of the Mississippi River to find a better life.

Butch Cassidy
1866–1909

Pearl Hart
1871–1925

Billy the Kid
1859–1881

Sundance Kid
1867–1908

Together, these trouble makers were responsible for over $250,000 stolen money and countless hours of police work.

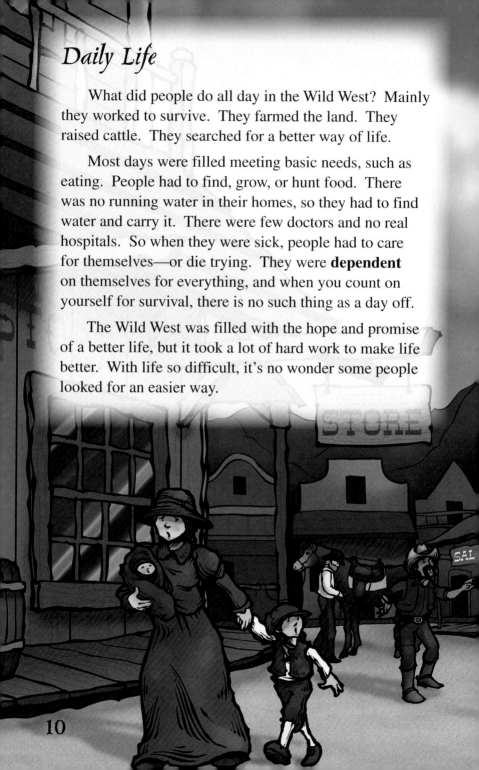

Daily Life

What did people do all day in the Wild West? Mainly they worked to survive. They farmed the land. They raised cattle. They searched for a better way of life.

Most days were filled meeting basic needs, such as eating. People had to find, grow, or hunt food. There was no running water in their homes, so they had to find water and carry it. There were few doctors and no real hospitals. So when they were sick, people had to care for themselves—or die trying. They were **dependent** on themselves for everything, and when you count on yourself for survival, there is no such thing as a day off.

The Wild West was filled with the hope and promise of a better life, but it took a lot of hard work to make life better. With life so difficult, it's no wonder some people looked for an easier way.

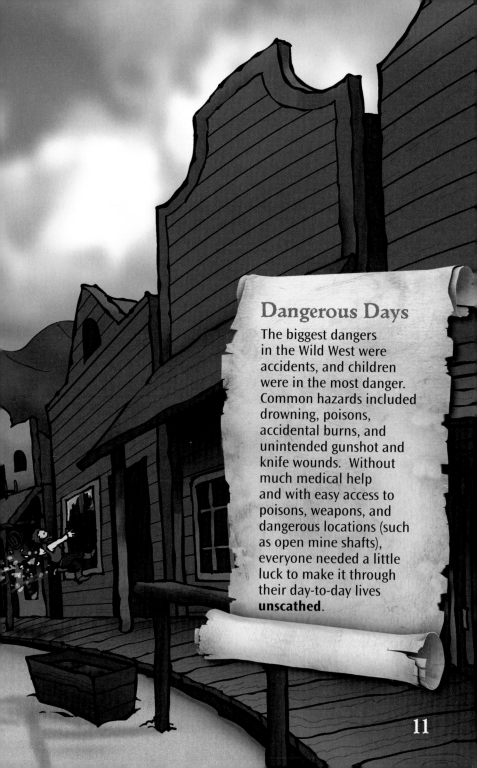

Dangerous Days

The biggest dangers in the Wild West were accidents, and children were in the most danger. Common hazards included drowning, poisons, accidental burns, and unintended gunshot and knife wounds. Without much medical help and with easy access to poisons, weapons, and dangerous locations (such as open mine shafts), everyone needed a little luck to make it through their day-to-day lives **unscathed**.

Survival

What did it take to survive in the Wild West? Just like today, most people wanted to work hard enough to make a better life for themselves and their children. But also like today, some people wanted an easier way. Life can be hard, and just taking what you need or pushing other people out of the way can seem like the better way to go.

Circuit Judge

In the Wild West, judges were few and far between. Judges traveled from town to town to put suspected criminals on trial.

But is it? Is being bad a choice, or are some people born bad? Maybe they can't figure out a better way. Maybe they are lazy. Or maybe they are **desperate**. And just how bad were the bad guys and gals of the Wild West? You be the judge!

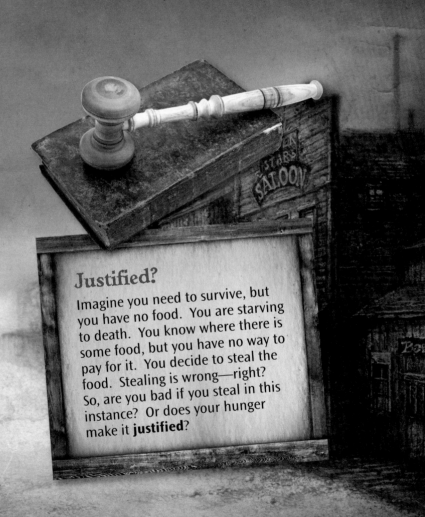

Justified?

Imagine you need to survive, but you have no food. You are starving to death. You know where there is some food, but you have no way to pay for it. You decide to steal the food. Stealing is wrong—right? So, are you bad if you steal in this instance? Or does your hunger make it **justified**?

WHAT DO YOU THINK?

What is wrong or right, and how do you know? Take a look at each of these situations and judge for yourself. Should you punish 'em up or let 'em go?

The Cheat

J.J. studied hard for the big test, but on test day, he froze. He knew the answers—but he just couldn't get his brain to work! Desperately, he looked at C.C.'s test. At first it seemed like gibberish, but then whew! Something clicked and he remembered everything he knew. He finished the test.

The Fighter

K's school has a strict no-fighting policy. No fighting, no matter what! One day as school was getting out, she saw a younger, smaller kid being pushed and bullied by a couple bigger kids. She got mad, and without thinking, she walked right over to the big kids and gave each of them a hard push. She told them they were bullies and she wasn't going to put up with it. One of the kids pushed K back, so K just let him have it. Just then, the principal walked by and saw K swing.

14

STOP! THINK...

- Is J.J. a cheat? Should K be punished? Was D wrong to steal it?

- What questions could you ask the suspects to make your decision?

- How would you feel if you were on trial for a crime you committed? What about a crime you didn't commit?

The Thief

D went to school hungry this morning. In fact, D went to school hungry most mornings. His parents were out of work and they could barely get by. D's hunger made him tired and he had trouble concentrating on schoolwork. All the kids' lunch bags were lined up outside the classroom door while the kids played on the playground before school started. D couldn't help himself—he grabbed a bag and ran around the corner to eat everything inside.

Jesse James

Among the most notorious **outlaws** of the Wild West, Jesse Woodson James was born the son of a preacher. He and his brother Frank fought for the Confederates during the Civil War. Some say it was the poor treatment they received from Union soldiers that turned them bad. Whatever the cause, they became some of the most famous criminals of their day, boldly robbing banks in broad daylight and holding up **stagecoaches** and trains. It was dangerous business. Sometimes, people were even killed.

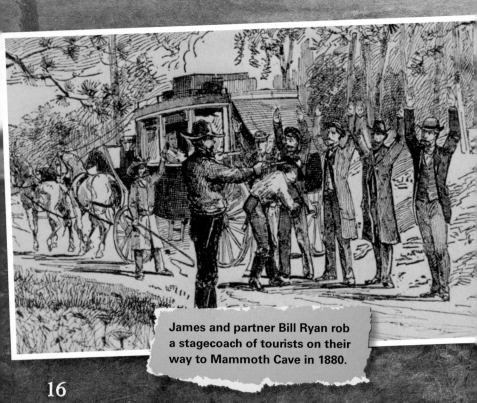

James and partner Bill Ryan rob a stagecoach of tourists on their way to Mammoth Cave in 1880.

WANTED
DEAD OR ALIVE

James was born in Missouri on September 5, 1847. He was shot to death by one of his own gang members on April 3, 1882.

SHERIFF

A Nation Divided

The American Civil War was waged between the northern and southern states from 1861 to 1865. Union soldiers fought in the North. Confederate soldiers fought in the South.

The Last Robbery

The James brothers and their gang had a successful run for many years, but things turned bad when they tried to rob a bank in 1876. The people of the town fought back and all the gang, except Jesse and Frank, were killed, injured, or captured.

Cole Younger, Jesse James, Bob Younger, Frank James (left to right)

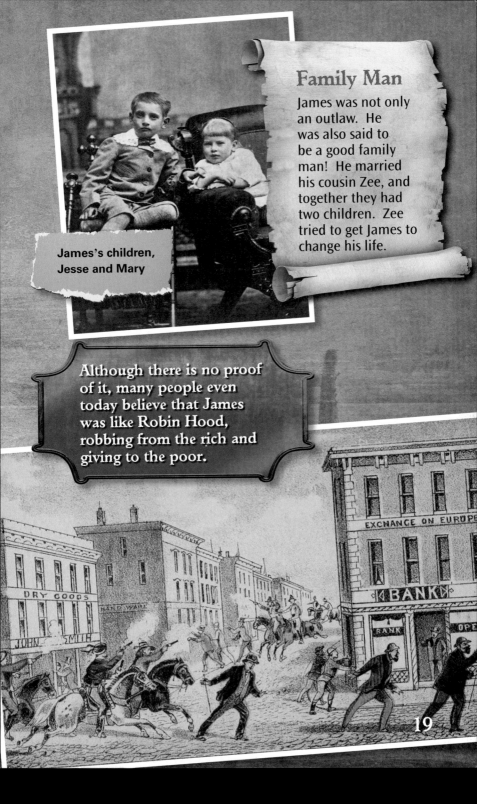

Family Man

James was not only an outlaw. He was also said to be a good family man! He married his cousin Zee, and together they had two children. Zee tried to get James to change his life.

James's children, Jesse and Mary

Although there is no proof of it, many people even today believe that James was like Robin Hood, robbing from the rich and giving to the poor.

Betrayal

Both brothers tried to live a different life, but they were **legendary** criminals. A large **bounty** was placed on James, and his friends were urged to capture him and turn him in. His "good friend" Robert Ford did just that on April 3, 1882—not that James would know it. He was shot dead from behind by Ford.

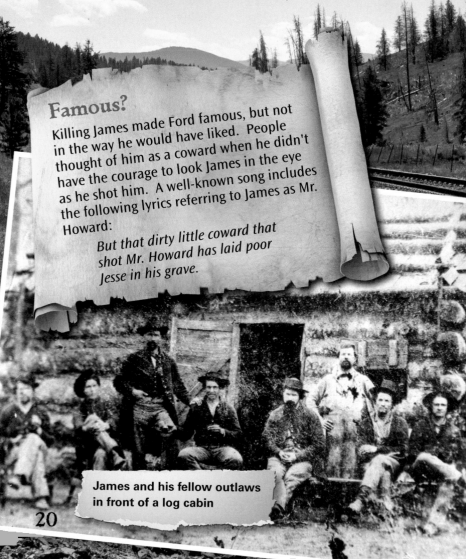

Famous?

Killing James made Ford famous, but not in the way he would have liked. People thought of him as a coward when he didn't have the courage to look James in the eye as he shot him. A well-known song includes the following lyrics referring to James as Mr. Howard:

But that dirty little coward that shot Mr. Howard has laid poor Jesse in his grave.

James and his fellow outlaws in front of a log cabin

The Man Who Did Him In

Ford was James's close friend. Or not. The $10,000 bounty on James was more than Ford could resist. One day, as James stopped to straighten a picture in James's home, Ford shot James in the back of his head. Ford only received a small portion of the reward. And he was nearly hanged for murder. But he was pardoned since it was "The Law" that asked him to do it in the first place.

PROCLAMATION
OF THE
GOVERNOR OF MISSOURI!
REWARDS
FOR THE ARREST OF
Express and Train Robbers.

STATE OF MISSOURI,}
EXECUTIVE DEPARTMENT.

WHEREAS, It has been made known to me, as the Governor of the State of Missouri, that certain parties, whose names are to me unknown, have confederated and banded themselves together for the purpose of committing robberies and other depredations within this State : and

WHEREAS, Said parties did, on or about the Eighth day of October, 1879, stop a train near Glendale, in the county of Jackson, in said State, and, with force and violence, take, steal and carry away the money and other express matter being carried thereon : and

WHEREAS, On the Eleventh day of July, 1881, said parties did with force and violence, take, steal, and carry away the money and other express matter being carried thereon ; and, in perpetration of the robbery last aforesaid, the parties engaged therein did kill and murder one WILLIAM WESTFALL, the conductor of the train, together with one JOHN McCULLOCH, who was at the time in the employ of said company, then on said train : and

WHEREAS, FRANK JAMES and JESSE W. JAMES stand indicted in the Circuit Court of said Daviess County, for the murder of JOHN W. SHEETS, and the parties engaged in the robberies and murders aforesaid have fled from justice and have absconded and secreted themselves :

NOW, THEREFORE, in consideration of the premises, and in lieu of all other rewards heretofore offered for the arrest or conviction of the parties aforesaid, or either of them, by any person or corporation, I, THOMAS T. CRITTENDEN, Governor of the State of Missouri, do hereby offer a reward of five thousand dollars ($5,000.00) for the arrest and conviction of each person participating in either of the robberies or murder, aforesaid, excepting the said FRANK JAMES and JESSE W. JAMES, and for the arrest and delivery of said

FRANK JAMES and JESSE W. JAMES,

and each or either of them, to the sheriff of said Daviess County, I hereby offer a reward of five thousand dollars, ($5,000.00,) and for the conviction of either of the parties last aforesaid of par- robberies above mentioned, I hereby offer a further reward of five thousand dollars, ($5,000.00.)

IN TESTI.......

By the Governor;
MICH'L.........

a poster offering a reward for the arrest of Frank and Jesse James, issued by the governor of Missouri in 1881

Belle Starr

Belle Starr sounds like the name of a celebrity, and she was—but not because of her great talents. It was her life of crime that made Starr a household name. Or was she just a victim of association?

Born Myra Maybelle Shirley, but called Belle, Starr was given an excellent education as a child and trained as a classical pianist. The Civil War was hard on her family, though, and they were forced to move from Missouri to Texas when the war came near their home.

Belle Starr

Starr was said to wear two pistols with extra cartridge belts at her hips.

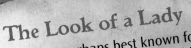

The Look of a Lady

Starr was perhaps best known for her style. She was often seen wearing a black velvet riding **habit** with a large feather in her hat. Like fine ladies of the day, she rode her horse **sidesaddle**.

A Crime Family

In Texas, Starr met and married Jim Reed. At first, they lived a quiet life with their two children, but Reed fell in with a gang of criminals. Starr objected to his life of crime, and she left him. Soon after, Reed was killed and Starr was left penniless.

She didn't escape a life of crime when she married Sam Starr, another thief. She learned how to rob and steal with her new husband and his family. She also often let known criminals stay in her home. Some say she didn't want to do it, and **harboring** criminals may have been her final downfall.

front cover of the Starr biography by Richard K. Fox, 1889

REWARD
☞ $10,000 ☜
IN GOLD COIN

Will be paid by the U.S. Gove[rnment]
for the apprehension

DEAD OR ALIV[E]
of

SAM and BELLE STARR

Wanted for Robbery Murder, Treason
and other acts ag[ainst the] peace

Often the only way the government could stop criminals was to offer a large reward.

Sam Starr

Belle Starr

Her Last Breath

Sam Starr was also killed. Belle quickly fell in love with another man, but that ended just as fast. Starr married, harbored, and worked with outlaws for years.

It was probably one of these criminals who ended her life. She had made a man named Edgar Watson angry by refusing to let him rent her land. It's also possible that her own children or husband did it, since they were feuding, too. No one knows for sure. They just know that two gunshots struck her down. Belle Starr, known for her flash and style, died in a pool of blood, lying on an old dirt road.

Starr and Blue Duck, one of Starr's boyfriends

Belle Starr escapes on horseback after being arrested.

SALOON

JAMES S

GROCERIES

How a Legend Is Made

There are many stories about Belle Starr, but most of them cannot be proven. Phony diaries and letters were published after her death. There was also a very popular book about her life that was published the year she died. The stories from all of these sources were told as truth and mixed with the real facts of her life. She was probably not the happy-go-lucky, gun-toting, rabble-rousing, party girl the stories say. More likely, she became a thief out of association and desperation and, once in, found herself unable to get out.

Doc Holliday

Was Doc Holliday a criminal—or just a **gambler** who was deadly with a **six-gun**? Born John Henry Holliday, Doc became a dentist at 21. He was also a highly-skilled **marksman**.

The O.K. Corral

Holliday may be best known for his friendship with Wyatt Earp and the famed "Gunfight at the O.K. Corral," perhaps the most famous gunfight in the Wild West. The fight was between the Earp brothers, who were "The Law," and the Clanton gang, who were called "cowboys." The O.K. Corral in Tombstone, Arizona, was the site of their most intense battle.

gunfight at the O.K. Corral

WANTED

Holliday was born in Griffin, Georgia, on August 14, 1851. He died a slow death in Colorado, dying on November 8, 1887, at the age of 36.

Taking a Gamble

When he was just 22, Holliday became sick with **tuberculosis** and moved to the Wild West in the hope that the climate would help him. He set up a dental practice, but patients didn't want to go to a dentist who coughed all the time. Holliday took up gambling to make money, and he was pretty good at it. But he also used his gun to get out of some of the bad situations that came with all that gambling.

Wyatt Earp

Wyatt Earp and Holliday became friends after Holliday saved Earp's life in a gunfight. Earp was a famous lawman.

Cowboys

In Tombstone, Arizona, the term *cowboy* was an insult. Cowboys were seen as bandits and horse and cattle thieves. *Cowboy* was almost another word for *outlaw*.

Dying Young

Holliday is known to have killed at least three people. But was he a "bad guy" or just a good guy with a gun in bad situations? Either way, he died young like so many gunmen; only it was his disease, not weapons, that killed him.

Holliday was told he had only a few months to live when he was diagnosed with tuberculosis, but he lived about 14 more years.

Originally built as a hotel in 1880, this building burned to the ground in 1882 and was rebuilt as Big Nose Kate's saloon.

Big Nose Kate

Mary Katherine Horony Cummings came to the United States with her family when she was 10. After her parents died, she and her siblings lived as foster children. Kate made her way to the Wild West, doing whatever she needed to survive. She got her unflattering nickname, Big Nose Kate, there. She also met Holliday and became his **common-law wife**. Kate was part of many of Holliday's exploits.

Big Nose Kate was born in Hungary on November 7, 1850. She lived to be nearly 90 years old.

Billy the Kid

William Henry McCarty Jr. was a small, sweet boy who was known for being polite and helpful. Raised by his mother and stepfather, young Billy was taken in by a neighboring family when his mother died. No one knows exactly why Billy turned to a life of crime, but some say his small size made him become extra tough to survive. We do know that he was forced to leave his **foster family** when he became too much for them to handle. Billy turned to crime and lived a life of lawlessness until his death.

Billy the Kid

Billy was known for his intelligence, skill with a gun, great sense of humor, and large front teeth.

Billy the Kid tried to make an honest living as a cook. He didn't last long.

a Colt revolver similar to the one used by Billy the Kid

Aw, Shucks

It was said that Billy became a thief to survive, but unlike many other bad guys of the time, Billy wasn't only a thief—he was a murderer. He was reported to have killed 27 men, although it's likely a lesser number. Still, many people say that those killings were mainly committed in self defense or done to correct a wrong.

Despite this, Billy became something of a folk hero. It seems he was very likable. People admired his skill and his quickness, and for some, it was easy to forget that he was also a killer. He got the nickname "the Kid" because of his youth and charm. People just liked him!

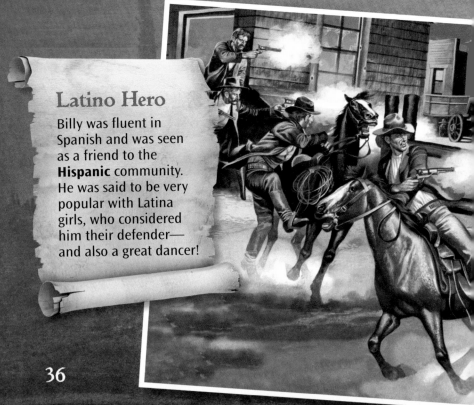

Latino Hero

Billy was fluent in Spanish and was seen as a friend to the **Hispanic** community. He was said to be very popular with Latina girls, who considered him their defender— and also a great dancer!

REWARD

($5,000.00)

Reward for the capture, dead or alive,
of one Wm. Wright, better known as

"BILLY THE KID"

Age, 18. Height, 5 feet, 3 i...
Weight, 125 lbs. Light hair...
eyes and eve... features. ...
the leader of ...rst band ...
desperadoes the ...
ever had to deal with. ...
reward will be paid for his c...
or positive proof of his death.

JIM DALTON, Sh...

DEAD OR ALIVE!
"BILLY THE KID

The High Cost of Fame

An 1880 bounty on Billy the Kid's
head made him famous. He was
mainly unknown before that time.

Amazing Escape

Before their final meeting, Billy notoriously escaped from one of Sheriff Pat Garrett's captures, despite being locked in a cell with two armed guards. Although it's not clear exactly how he did it, it is known that somehow he got his hands on a gun, killed both guards, and managed to free himself from shackles before escaping on a stolen horse.

A Dark Demise

Billy met his end at the hands of Garrett. Garrett tracked the outlaw for many years, and Billy escaped from him more than once. But finally, Billy unintentionally walked into a building where Garrett was hiding in the darkness. Billy said, "Quien es?" (Spanish for "Who is it?") and Garrett shot Billy to death.

Billy the Kid meets his end at the hands of Sheriff Pat Garrett in Fort Sumner, New Mexico.

Butch Cassidy and The Sundance Kid

Robert Leroy Parker left his home and family when he was just a young teenager and went to work on a dairy farm. There, he worked with Mike Cassidy, who was a horse and cattle **rustler** on the side. But Parker idolized Cassidy and saw him as a **mentor**, eventually using Cassidy's last name as his own.

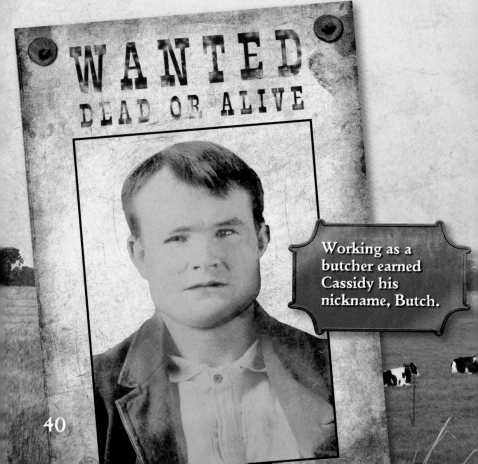

WANTED
DEAD OR ALIVE

> Working as a butcher earned Cassidy his nickname, Butch.

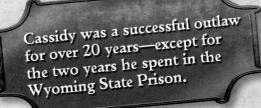

Cassidy was a successful outlaw for over 20 years—except for the two years he spent in the Wyoming State Prison.

First Crime

Cassidy's first criminal act was stealing some pie and a pair of jeans from a shop. He left an **IOU** note that said he would come back to pay. But the shop owner pressed charges, and it went to trial. Cassidy was cleared.

Partners in Crime

Mike Cassidy introduced the young man to thievery, and the young Cassidy grew to like it. He committed more and more crimes and even started his own gang called the Wild Bunch. They mainly robbed and stole, but also killed, and they became both famous and feared.

In time, Cassidy welcomed a young man named Harry, nicknamed the Sundance Kid, into the gang. Butch and Sundance became true partners in crime.

the Wild Bunch train robbers: (standing left to right) Bill Carver, Kid Curry, (seated left to right) Sundance Kid, Ben Kilpatrick, and Cassidy

Laura Bullion

Laura Bullion was the daughter of outlaws, the long-time girlfriend of an outlaw, and an outlaw in the Wild Bunch. She led a life as lawless as the rest of them and even served many years in jail. The difference between her and most of her partners is that Bullion lived a long life after her years of crime. She worked as a **seamstress** for many years and died in 1961 at about the age of 85.

Bullion was also known as The Rose of the Wild Bunch.

Running from the Law

As their criminal activity grew, so did pressure from The Law. Cassidy and the Sundance Kid had to keep moving, because The Law was always close on their heels. The pair fled to South America, where they continued their outlaw activities.

Cassidy and the Sundance Kid hold up a Union Pacific Railroad train.

Etta Place

For many years, the Sundance Kid had one steady girlfriend who may have been his wife. Etta Place was the name given to his female partner, but the name was chosen by lawmen only because a name was needed for the wanted posters! No one really knows who she was, what her real name was, or what happened to her.

The Sundance Kid's real name was Harry Alonzo Longbaugh. He took the name Sundance after he was imprisoned in the town of Sundance in 1887.

the Sundance Kid and Etta Place

Finally, trapped in a small cabin, the police surrounded the duo, firing rounds of bullets through the walls. Screams were heard and then two single shots. When the firing stopped, Cassidy and the Sundance Kid were found dead, covered in bullet holes—with one in each of their skulls. Their legendary crime spree was at an end.

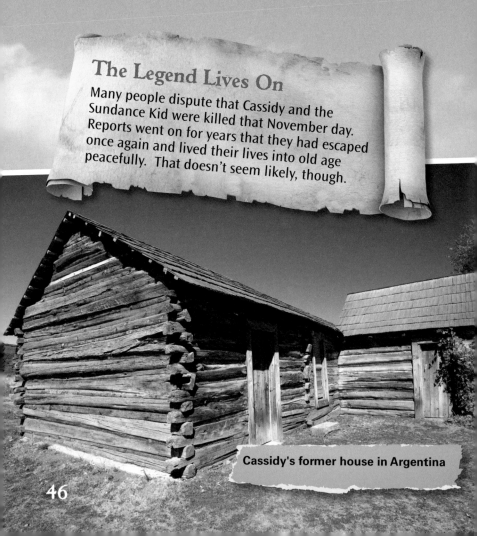

The Legend Lives On

Many people dispute that Cassidy and the Sundance Kid were killed that November day. Reports went on for years that they had escaped once again and lived their lives into old age peacefully. That doesn't seem likely, though.

Cassidy's former house in Argentina

Photograph of **GEORGE PARKER.**

Description.

NAME. GEORGE PARKER, alias "BUTCH" CASSIDY, alias GEORGE CASSIDY, alias INGERFIELD.

AGE, 36 years (1901).

WEIGHT, 165 lbs.

COMPLEXION, light.

EYES, blue.

NATIONALITY, American.

HEIGHT, 5 ft., 9 inches.

BUILD, Medium.

COLOR OF HAIR, flaxen.

MUSTACHE, sandy, if any.

OCCUPATION, cowboy, rustler.

CRIMINAL OCCUPATION, bank robber and highwayman, cattle and horse thief.

MARKS, two cuts scars back of head, small scar under left eye, small brown mole calf of leg.

"BUTCH" CASSIDY is known as a criminal principally in Wyoming, Utah, Idaho, Colorado and Nevada and has served time in Wyoming State penitentiary at Laramie for grand larceny, but was pardoned January 19th, 1896.

Description of HARRY LONGBAUGH.

NAME. HARRY LONGBAUGH, alias "KID" LONGBAUGH, alias HARRY ALONZO.

AGE, 35 to 40 years.

COMPLEXION, dark (looks like quarter breed Indian).

EYES, black.

FEATURES, Grecian type.

HEIGHT, 5 ft. 9 inches.

COLOR OF HAIR, black.

MUSTACHE, if any, black.

NATIONALITY, American.

WEIGHT, 165 to 170 lbs.

BUILD, rather slim.

NOSE, rather long.

OCCUPATION, cowboy, rustler.

CRIMINAL OCCUPATION, highwayman and bank burglar, cattle and horse thief.

HARRY LONGBAUGH served 18 months in jail at Sundance, Cook Co., Wyoming, when a boy, for horse stealing. In December, 1892, HARRY LONGBAUGH, Bill Madden and Harry Bass "held up" a Great Northern train at Malta, Montana. Bass and Madden were tried for this crime, convicted and sentenced to 10 and 14 years respectively; LONGBAUGH escaped and since has been a fugitive. June 28, 1897, under the name of Frank Jones, Longbaugh participated with Harvey Logan, alias Curry, Tom Day and Walter Putney, in the Belle Fouche, S. D., bank robbery. All were arrested, but Longbaugh and Harvey Logan escaped from jail at Deadwood, October 31, 1897, and have not since been arrested.

GEORGE PARKER, alias "BUTCH" CASSIDY, [...]AUGH and a third man were implicated in the robbery of the First National Bank, [...] 9, 1900.

Cassidy's and the Sundance Kid's file from the Pinkerton National Detective Agency

Murder and Suicide?

Many people think that during the final shootout, one of the partners was wounded so badly that the other partner put a bullet in his brain to put him out of his misery. He then turned the gun on himself.

Pearl Hart

Pearl Taylor was born to wealthy parents and had a good upbringing. At 16, she fell in love with a young man with the last name of Hart and eloped with him, but he was abusive. She left her husband and tried to make it alone many times. But being alone was difficult. She returned to her husband when going it alone was not successful.

Hart was born around 1871 in Lindsay, Ontario, Canada. She died some time after 1925.

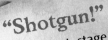

"Shotgun!"

In the west, stage coach drivers could easily be attacked, so someone was often hired to sit next to the driver to hold a shotgun and watch for robbers. That's why today "calling shotgun" means sitting next to the driver. Hart conducted some of the most famous stagecoach robberies in history.

This 1909 N.C. Wyeth painting depicts a stagecoach driver and "shotguns."

A Dark Heart

Hart's mother became ill, and Hart wanted to be with her. Since she had no money, Hart and her friend, Joe Boot, decided to rob a stagecoach. Hart cut her hair short and dressed like a man, which was highly unusual for the time. She became notorious as a female stagecoach robber, which was also rare.

Stories of women dressed as men and robbing stagecoaches shocked newspaper readers.

Hart's stagecoach robbery on May 30, 1899, is one of the last recorded stagecoach robberies in the United States. It wasn't many years later that people started trading coaches and wagons for automobiles!

cowgirl Pearl Hart

Hart and Boot were captured about a week after the robbery. He was sentenced to 30 years in prison, but she got only 5 years. She was pardoned in 1902.

The Bandit Queen

Hart lived out her life mainly in private, other than a brief time as an act in Buffalo Bill's Wild West Show. She was last seen in 1925, and no one knows where or when she died.

Buffalo Bill's Wild West Show

Former soldier and hunter William Frederick Cody, called Buffalo Bill, opened a traveling show featuring cowboys and western entertainment. Hart appeared briefly in the show. She was known as the Bandit Queen and reenacted her stagecoach robbery.

Cattle Kate

Ellen Liddy Watson, known as Cattle Kate, was a successful rancher in Wyoming. She was even able to set up her own **cattle brand**. Other ranchers didn't like her success. They harassed her and accused her of cattle rustling. Riders were sent to arrest her. They arrested her—and hanged her without a trial. Bad gal of the Wild West? More like a good gal caught in a bad situation.

Cattle Kate was born on July 2, 1861, in Ontario, Canada. She was hanged on July 20, 1889.

THE LAW

For every bad guy in the Wild West, there were plenty of good guys. They served as The Law, and here are just a few of them.

Roy Bean

Justice of the Peace Roy Bean served in Texas, where he held court in his saloon. He called himself The Law West of the Pecos. He is remembered as a hanging judge, but he only actually sentenced two men to hanging. Strangely, he himself was almost hanged as a young man by the friends of a man he killed in a duel. The near **lynching** left Bean with a permanent neck problem. Ouch!

Why So Many Bad Guys?

The Wild West was filled mainly with men and a few women and children. Throughout time, places with mainly men have tended to have more crime than other places. There was also a lot of gambling and drinking in the Wild West, which made tempers flare. All these things added to the overall troubles and crime there.

Isaac Parker

Called the Hanging Judge, Judge Isaac Parker served for 21 years. He took his job very seriously. In his service, he presided as judge in nearly 13,500 cases and convicted almost 9,500 people. He sentenced 160 of those people to death by hanging.

Bat Masterson

Barclay "Bat" Masterson was an army scout and saloonkeeper before becoming a policeman and then sheriff, working with Wyatt Earp. He was famous for capturing several notorious criminals. Masterson also got the attention of President Theodore Roosevelt, who became his friend and appointed him as a deputy United States Marshal.

Wyatt Earp

After some tough early years in which he was on the wrong side of The Law, Wyatt Earp traveled to a variety of **boomtowns** and became a lawman there. He is most known for the gunfight at the O.K. Corral, in which three lawbreakers were killed and only Earp came away uninjured. Today, Earp is remembered as one of the best and toughest lawmen of the Wild West.

Right or Wrong?

Good or bad? It's a tricky question. It may be as simple as knowing the law. Good is always on the right side of The Law. Isn't it?

Throughout time, people have tried to figure out what is good and what is bad. Chances are, the question of good and bad will exist as long as there are guys and gals and choices to be made. Just like the folks in the Wild West, you may have to figure it out for yourself.

Judge Roy Bean listening as a horse thief stands trial

Hoodoo Brown

Hymen G. Neill, called Hoodoo Brown, worked both sides of The Law. He led the notorious Dodge City Gang that ran the **politics** of Las Vegas, New Mexico. He was a lawman and **coroner**, and he used his positions to cover up his gang's crimes. He also worked to rid his town of criminals while at the same time living as a criminal himself. No one knows for sure what happened to Hoodoo Brown, but his legend lives on.

Glossary

barons—people with great power and wealth

boomtowns—towns that grow quickly

bounty—money given as a reward for capturing a criminal

cattle brand—a technique for marking livestock so as to identify the owner

common-law wife—a woman who becomes a wife not through a legal contract but instead by living as a wife over a period of time

coroner—an officer of the court who investigates deaths not caused by natural events

deceiving—false; not what something seems

dependent—relying on someone or something else

desperate—having an urgent need or hopeless feelings

established—set or settled

foster family—people who raise children who are orphaned, neglected, or delinquent

frontier—the outer edge of a civilized or settled part of a country

gambler—a person who plays a game of chance for money or other stakes

habit—a costume worn for horseback riding

harboring—giving a home and support to

Hispanic—related to or being a person living in the United States from or whose ancestors were from Latin America

instincts—natural impulses that occur without thought or planning

IOU—a paper that acknowledges a debt, an acronym for the words *I owe you*

justified—acceptable or guiltless because of cause

legendary—well-known, famous

lynching—to put someone to death illegally, usually by hanging, and mainly done by a group or mob

marksman—a person skilled in aiming and shooting a gun

mentor—a person who trains and supports another usually younger and less experienced person, especially in a particular skill or career

notorious—well-known for unfavorable or negative reasons

outlaws—people who act outside the rule of law

pioneers—the people who are the first to explore and settle in an area

politics—the science or art of government

rustler—a thief, especially of cattle and horses

seamstress—a person who sews or tailors clothes

sidesaddle—a saddle for women in which the rider sits with both legs on one side of the horse

six-gun—a six-chambered revolver

stagecoaches—coaches that carry passengers or mail and are pulled by horses

tuberculosis—an infectious disease, mainly of the lungs, once also called *consumption*

unscathed—untouched or unharmed

Index

Bibliography

King, David C. *Wild West Days: Discover the Past with Fun Projects, Games, Activities, and Recipes.* **John Wiley & Sons, 1998.**

Join three kids in Wyoming Territory in the year 1878. You'll learn what daily life was really like in the Wild West by playing fun games, making your own toys and crafts, and doing everyday work just like kids of the past. Activities include cooking sourdough flapjacks, keeping a pioneer diary, and making a lariat.

Linz, Kathi. *Chickens May Not Cross the Road and Other Crazy (But True) Laws.* **Sandpiper, 2007.**

Discover crazy laws that either still are, or once were, in state law books. Colorful illustrations show just how silly some of these laws really are.

Martin, Gayle. *Gunfight at the O.K. Corral: Luke and Jenny Visit Tombstone.* **Five Star Publications, 2009.**

Follow Luke and Jenny's historical adventure at the O.K. Corral. This brother and sister duo may be fictional, but they will introduce you to the real people and events of the famous gunfight—the Earp brothers and Doc Holliday versus the Clantons and McLaurys!

Murray, Stuart. *Wild West.* **DK Publishing, Incorporated, 2005.**

Journey to the American West and see how pioneers, cowboys, and cavalry won the frontier. Discover how to pan for gold and take a ride on the Pony Express. You'll meet outlaws, lawmen, and even snake oil salesmen.

Sheinkin, Steve. *Which Way to the Wild West?* **Square Fish, 2010.**

This book offers you a history of the American West "with the good bits put back." Humorous storytelling and illustrations make learning about the adventures, discoveries, dirty deeds, and fearless people of the Wild West a blast.

More to Explore

Buffalo Bill's Wild West Show
http://www.buffalobill.com/originalIndex.html

Learn about Colonel William F. Cody and how he began Buffalo Bill's Wild West show. Meet the Montana family and performers that continue the show's tradition. You can also see old posters from the show.

Butch Cassidy and the Sundance Kid Rob a Train, 1899
http://www.eyewitnesstohistory.com/cassidy.htm

Experience a train robbery by Butch Cassidy and the Sundance Kid through the eyes of a mail clerk working on the Union Pacific Railroad. See photographs of the outlaws and the train car they blew up.

Cowboys Quiz
http://quizzes-for-kids.com/history/cowboys-quiz

Test your knowledge of famous Wild West cowboys, from Buffalo Bill and Jesse James to Doc Holliday and Billy the Kid. Then, continue the challenge with another Quiz About Cowboys.

PBS Kids Go! WayBack Gold Rush
http://pbskids.org/wayback/goldrush

Travel back in time and join the California Gold Rush. Catch Gold Fever, journey with the Forty-Niners, and meet a cast of characters just like the people who lived during the Gold Rush. You can also visit the Joke Space to read or send in your own American history jokes.

The Wild West
http://www.thewildwest.org

Meet the outlaws, lawmen, and women of the Wild West, and relive the exciting gunfight at the O.K. Corral. You'll learn about American Indians, as well as movie cowboys, cowboy songs, and cowboy recipes. You can also play online shoot 'em up games and solve Wild West jigsaw puzzles.

About the Author

Dona Herweck Rice grew up in Anaheim, California, and graduated from the University of Southern California with a degree in English and from the University of California at Berkeley with a credential for teaching. She has been a teacher in preschool through tenth grade, a researcher, a librarian, and a theater director. She is now an editor, a poet, a writer of teacher materials, and a writer of books for children. She is married with two sons and lives in Southern California, where she tries to be good.